Broken

to

Chosen

Joy Lasher

Broken to Chosen

ISBN-13: 9798688050158

Copyright © 2020 by Joy Lasher

Cover Design: Michael Maris

Foreword

I have known Joy for a few years and reading her life story is a must for anyone. I have so much respect for Joy in all kinds of areas, but the one thing that sticks out to me is how real and authentic she is. I was able to be part of her journey of freedom, healing and restoration. I have seen her walk out these areas and I can honestly say she is a woman of truth. She is so full of life and overflows with Jesus. Knowing who she is now and reading her past it doesn't seem like she's the same person. She has allowed God to do such a work in her spirit, soul, and body. God is no respecter of persons. He can change and transform your life just like He did hers. Your story may not be just like hers, but your transformation is just one relationship away. I pray her story opens your heart to God and that you invite Him in to heal whatever needs to be made whole. You are not here by accident. God has incredible plans for your life. You may feel broken, but God says you are chosen. Thank you Joy for being so transparent and honest. Your life has already and will continue to touch many people.

Lindsey Bussey
Associate Pastor & Life Group Coordinator
Life United
Shreveport, LA

A Letter from the Author

During the COVID-19 pandemic quarantine of 2020, the Lord put it on my heart to write this book for you which is a memoir of my life. It is a book about struggle and perseverance. But it is also a book about hope, love, finding your identity in Christ, your calling, healing, faith, and restoration through the Lord Jesus Christ.

The world is a hurting and broken world and I believe my story is something that needs to be shared so others can find freedom. I pray this book encourages you in knowing you are not alone. There are others out there who have gone through the same things as you. And while you might feel broken right now. Know that there is hope in and through Jesus Christ for a new life! The enemy wants you to stay broken, but God says rise up, YOU ARE CHOSEN!

Joy Lasher

Table of Contents

Foreword

Introduction

Ch 1. From the Beginning

Ch 2. Everything Fell Apart

Ch 3. The Struggle Continues

Ch 4. A Fresh Start

Ch 5. Believing for the Impossible

Ch 6. The Healing Journey Begins

Ch 7. Changed in A Moment

Ch 8. God's Not Done

Ch 9. Restoration

Ch 10. We Are Just Getting Started

Ch 11. Your Journey Begins

Resources

About the Author

Contact

Introduction

It was May of 2019; I had just graduated from ministry school and the next day we moved across the United State to New Jersey for military orders. We had received a word from the Lord concerning our assignment here in the early spring of 2019 before the orders came. We came here believing for a new season of ministry only to find out it would be a season of waiting. Of course, my husband had been ministering several times a week where he was stationed previously with his church and with the prison ministry, so this made the transition quite difficult for him. It was also difficult for me, because I had all these ideas that I would move into ministry after graduating from ministry school and prophetic school.

We moved here and heard all these words about revival in the area, but it still did not really set a spark in us because we did not know what our part in it was. We pretty much came here and felt like we had to start over with everything.

Fast forward ten months later; we are now in the midst of the global COVID-19 pandemic. When this started, we did not see the big picture that God was doing. We decided to take time and really press into God through worship, the Word and prayer. We felt the Lord started to reveal to us that this was going to be a Passover season and there would be a great outpouring of His Spirit on all flesh just like the days of Pentecost. We knew we had to start praying for revival and a great awakening. I truly believe with all my heart that we are on the edge of a move of God unlike the church has ever seen. I believe we are in the last days and we are so close to the second coming of Christ! It really is such an exciting time to be alive in the body of Christ.

In this time, the Lord instructed my husband to write a book called "Walking in Fullness." I believe this book will help other born again Christians to learn how to walk in the fullness of God in these last days. Shortly, after my husband finished his book, I really felt the Lord instructed me to write a book about my journey of faith, healing, and restoration.

I believe in this time, the Lord is raising up a new generation of believers for the end time harvest and He is helping believers to get set free and walk in the freedom that Jesus paid for you on the cross. I pray this book imparts to you faith unlike every before, gives you revelation knowledge of who you are in Christ, your calling, and the love He has for you. The Father wants you to walk in healing, forgiveness, freedom and so much more. We have to deal with all of our stuff so we can get to a place where we are an open vessel for Him to use us in these last days to rise up and be the bold church we are called to be. Be encouraged by my journey the Lord wants me to share with you.

Chapter 1

From the beginning

When I look back at my life, I can now see that the enemy started attacking me from an early age to alter my trust of others, my view of my heavenly Father and to distort my identity.

When I was a little girl, we would attend church on Sunday and then a different church the next Sunday and so on. I do not recall being rooted in a real church family as we were always hopping around. I did attend Sunday school but never really understood what they were really talking about. Honestly, the best part was getting a donut! They had Southern Maid donuts every time I was there! They talked about the Bible but it seemed to me like a bunch of stories being told and people talked about Jesus but who was Jesus anyway? I did not really know. And I certainly did not have much of a relationship with Him. I knew that my mother was Christian, and I guess that made me Christian too! I had a Bible but seldomly read it and when I did, I did not really understand it.

Difficulties in my life started at a pretty young age. I remember my mother and father were separated and we moved to Louisiana from Ohio because my uncle lived there, and we had some family that we knew. Because my parents were separated, it was frowned upon at many churches we attended, hence our hopping around to churches. I remember my oldest brother lived with us for some time before moving out, joining the Navy, and getting married. My youngest brother was not around much. My youngest sister was born after we moved to Louisiana, making my mother a single mother raising two children on her own. I have memories of my mother when I was young working many odd jobs to provide for us. She was a great mother and we never knew we had any lack.

My father was present very little in my life. I remember seeing him three or four times when I was young, and it always impacted me in a negative manner. One time he came down and we were having dinner. My mother had made meatloaf and I did not want to eat it. I ended up throwing a fit and I was told to leave the table. My father then told me, "for a pretty smart girl you're pretty stupid." Another time he came down, we were playing a game of cards and I ended up winning the game. He got furious, stood up and threw the picnic table across the room from where we were sitting. Of course, I was scared and did not know what I had done or what to do. I had never seen someone get so angry before. I probably only saw my father one other time when I was young. I believe because of some of the instances that did occur with my father, my mother may have told him he could not see me anymore. I do not remember seeing him or speaking to him again till I was a teenager in high school.

Fast forward a couple years later, my mother had become friends with the neighbor across the street. One day at our home, I was playing video games and the son of the neighbor came over. He came and sat with me and watched me play video games. He then told me I needed to hit my reset button. I was confused and asked him why I would need to hit my reset button. He then proceeded to touch my privates and tell me that I needed to hit my reset button. Of course, I felt violated and jumped up and left. He did come back over to the house at a later point in time. I was outside and he started to come toward me. I was terrified because of what had already happened, so I began to run. He began to chase me around my mother's vehicle. I remember I had a cap gun and pointed it at him to shoot him. I think in the moment I thought it was a real gun and wanted to protect myself. It was later, that I did tell my mother of both instances. I remember them moving out of our neighborhood shortly after and I never saw him again. Of course, in this time, memories started to get hazy and lost. I believe I started to mentally shut down as a child to protect myself and went into survival mode. I went form a happy child to sad and depressed and could not understand why I felt that way. I believe it was due to a combination of events that happened, and that life would only get worse as it went on.

In middle school, I was honor student at the top of my class. I was in all the advanced classes and was also an esteemed basketball player. My coach was a Christian and I was part of the Fellowship of Christian Athletes. Of course, we prayed in the club and prayed before every game, but I still had no relationship with God or even knew who He really was. Playing basketball and academics kept me quite busy and kept my mind off things that had happened and things that were missing in my life. I excelled in everything I put my mind to and always went above and beyond. Even though I was successful, it did not seem like it was ever enough. Everyone around me told me how smart and successful I was but there always seemed like some part of me was missing.

I soon went on to high school where I continued to excel in sports and academics. It was in high school where I would come across some new friends. I met a guy in art class who I thought was cute and amazing. We became friends and spent a lot of time together. We became best friends and of course I thought it would develop into more than just friends. We did end up going to one of our school dances together. He later introduced me to a female friend of his who was quite older than us. We all began hanging out together. One night, we were all hanging out and they told me they had Vodka. They asked me if I wanted to drink and through peer pressure, I ended up trying alcohol for the first time in my life and I proceeded to get drunk. I remember we were all outside laying in the grass and the next thing I know I passed out. I woke up the next day at home and found a note in my pocket that she had wrote saying the guy who I really liked was gay. Of course, this really hurt my feelings and was quite shocking because I really liked him. He was the first person I really decided to let my guard down to and let in my life. I did confront him about it, and he told me it was true and that the only reason he dated me was to cover up the fact that he was gay. You could imagine how hurtful this would be to someone. I did not know how to really respond so I pushed my feelings down and felt bad for him. I decided to remain friends with them despite what had happened. After hanging out with them for a couple years, his friend and I started hanging out even more. Turns out she was gay as well and started to take a liking to me. I entertained the idea of a relationship with her and thought maybe I could be gay as well. It was one night that my mother came outside and found us in the car together making out. She dragged me out of the car and told me I would never see her again. Of course, that did not stop me at the time, I continued to see her in secret. She became very obsessive, controlling and began following me. When she saw me talking to a guy, she would get angry, drink, and spread rumors about me. One night she followed me home, she was drunk and attempted to go after my mother who was trying to protect me. It was in that moment, that I lost it on her, went after her and told her to get off our property. Months later, I wrote her a letter asking for forgiveness and told her I wanted to be with her. We ended up hanging out again but then things went downhill quickly. I decided to never see her again.

Early in my junior year, I was at a rock concert with a couple friends and felt the urge to call my mother and check on her. I called the house, but no one answered, and it just rang and rang. I felt in myself that something was not quite right, and I needed to get home right away. I asked my friends to drive me home. When I had arrived, it was extremely late, and I saw the weed eater just lying in the yard with the extension cord. I thought that was very unusual for my mother. I then noticed my neighbor came to meet me outside and proceeded to tell me my mother had had a massive stroke. I was in shock and they told me they were going to take me to the hospital right away. I remember getting to the hospital and my oldest brother was there to meet me. After I had spoken with my brother, I walked down the hall and saw my mother in the hospital room half paralyzed saying, "everything is going to be okay Joy". I remember in that moment I walked outside where my sister was, and I said to myself I must be strong, and I must be the mother now. I remember I never cried or showed any emotion. I put up a wall to become strong and continued in my survival mode that I had always known.

My mother was in the hospital for close to a year. My sister and I lived across the street with one of our neighbors for quite some time. Later my sister went to live with her dad, and I went to live with my oldest brother. Those were some exceedingly difficult times. I do not know if I ever voiced it, but I know I had thoughts of why would God have done this to us? Why would God do this to my mother who has done nothing but struggle to raise us up on her own? It did not seem fair. I thought we had already been through so much and I had already had so much happen to us, why this too? I had lots of questions and doubts and there was no one to bring me comfort or answers. I remember people would come up to us and say God was trying to teach us something through this. Or they would say that we had done something wrong. It did not make sense to me and I thought what kind of God would do this? Why would I want to know a God like this?

Right before my senior year, my mother came home from the hospital. My uncle and neighbor had built some ramps on the house and prepared the house for my mother's arrival. When she came home, she cried with joy and they lifted her down from the van in her wheelchair. I thought to myself that I must be strong now and take care of everyone. I knew everything in my life had totally changed. No one ever talked to us about what had happened to our mother. No one from the hospital ever came to us to show us how to do anything. We were children, now being forced to grow up quickly and learn how to take care of ourselves and our mother.

I started helping with my mother on a daily basis as I started my senior year of high school. I also started working at a local restaurant close to our home. I had to learn to drive and started driving my mother to work every day. She returned to work as a teacher's aide and was not there long until she was forced to leave by the teacher because she could not do her job fully as before. This was a huge disappointment for my mother, and I did not know where income was going to come from. During this time, I started going out and hanging out with a much older group of people. I began drinking a lot and even started smoking marijuana. This was the way I escaped from and stayed numb to all the things that had taken place. I managed to keep my grades up in hopes of receiving a scholarship to college.

Still hanging out with the older group of people, I met an older guy and took a liking to him. I thought he was the coolest guy I had ever met. He was part of a popular band, drank and smoked. We began spending more time together and things became intimate quickly. This was my first intimate encounter with a guy. A couple months later, one of his friends took a liking to me and decided to get me drunk one night. I believe there was some pills slipped to me as well and we ended up sleeping together. The guy I was dating caught wind of it and began calling me names all around town. Of course, I still pursued him in trying to get him back. In pursuing him, I was able to get him to sleep with me one more time. In this time, I was getting close to being able to graduate and had just received a full scholarship to the college of my choice. It was four weeks later, when my period did not come, that I realized after taking a pregnancy test, I was pregnant. I could not believe it and knew my mother would be so disappointed in me and have a fit. After all, I was supposed to be the first person in my family to go to college and here I was seventeen and pregnant. I decided to wait till after high school graduation. After graduation, I told my mother about the pregnancy and I made the decision right away to get an abortion. I thought there is no way I can go to college, take care of my mother, and take care of a baby and the guy who got me pregnant hates me. How would I do all of that and make money to support everyone? It seemed impossible to me. I went to the clinic and had my mother give authorization for me to have a pharmaceutical abortion, which they call the RU-486 abortion pill. Of course, the abortion clinic told me that if I did the abortion at ten weeks the baby was not alive and would not feel a thing. I thought what I was doing was a good thing and my baby would not feel anything because it was not even alive yet. I would come to find out years later, that this information was a lie!

After I had the abortion, I remember nothing was ever discussed with me regarding it. The only people who knew were my mother, a close friend and me. It was like it

never even took place. When a woman has an
abortion, the repercussions of her decision are
never discussed. There is no one who talks
with you about what you did or helps you deal
with it or heal from it. You are never told
how much it will really affect you long term.
It would take me the following fourteen years
to find this out.

Chapter 2

Everything Fell Apart

Shortly after having the abortion, I started my freshman year at a very prestigious college. I received a room and board scholarship as well and chose to live on campus. My first day I moved into my dorm, my roommate invited a bunch of people over to drink in the dorm. I did not partake but it was my room too, so I stayed there and just sat on my bed. Of course, it was reported, and we were ordered to go to court on campus for drinking, even though I was not involved. I thought to myself, "this is off to a really great start".

I had signed up for an intense class load and thought now that the abortion was behind me, I could handle it and focus on school. I thought wrong! A couple months into school, my grades were already suffering. I had a hard time even getting out of bed on a daily basis and suffered from depression, fatigue, and brain fog. At the time, I had no idea what was wrong with me, but I just kept trying to press through. After all, I had worked so hard my whole life for this very moment. I also wanted to make my family proud. I lost interest in class quickly and hated being around my roommate. I started hanging out with some old friends who were much older than I was. During that time, I began to take pills and cut myself daily to try to alleviate pain from the abortions. There was a lot of drinking and smoking marijuana for quite some time. Then, one night, a friend suggested us trying cocaine. I thought why not, what could it hurt; maybe it will make me feel better. In the moment cocaine seemed to make everything fade away and I could escape into a different realm of unreality. I thought this is great! Little did I know it would lead to other drugs. When we were unable to find any more cocaine, a friend suggested we try meth. Again, I thought why not, what could it hurt. We started doing meth on a regular basis. Of course, by this time I stopped going to class all together. I ended up moving off campus and moving back home to live with my mother to help with her. The meth use began to get out of control to where we were not sleeping for days at a time. I began to feel like I could not live without it. I also began to have fits of rage for no apparent reason. The meth use went on for almost a year and it got bad. I believe my mother began to see just how bad it had become in my life. One day I came home high, had not slept for days, and wanted to crash. Suddenly, my car was gone. Little did I know that my mother had plans to have me arrested for drug use.

The cops showed up at the house and of course I tried to escape but all the doors and window were locked. I decided to hide in the shower and hide all my drug paraphernalia. Despite my hiding, they found me and arrested me. It was probably one of the scariest and most shameful moments of my life. In that moment I was upset with my mother for having me arrested and could not understand why she would do that to me. I felt like my future was ruined.

I arrived at the intake facility where police officials questioned me for some time. They then took me to the local parish jail where I would await arraignment and then to be transferred to another facility. Upon arraignment, my brother purchased me a lawyer who would help to lower my bond and try to get me out of jail. After my arraignment, they transferred me to another facility an hour and a half away. I was in a large dorm with a couple hundred other woman.

At that moment, I was stripped of everything in my life: clothes, makeup, belongings, my family, money, identity, etc. I felt lost, shamed, embarrassed, angry, bitter, abandoned, depressed and more. I did not know if I would ever get out or what kind of life I would now have. I had been a good kid my whole life and had never gotten into trouble of any kind, but my life went from perfect to a disaster in the matter of a year.

It was in that jail where I met two Christian girls. For the first time in my life, I heard about who Jesus was and what He did for me on the cross. It was in that moment of desperation that it finally became living to me and I felt alive again. I remember a feeling of joy I had in jail after hearing about Jesus. I began to call my mom and talk to her about finding Jesus in jail. However, I never fully gave my life to Jesus and would soon abandon my newly found Jesus.

While I was in jail, I found out my mother had fallen and broke her hip. She had been at a rehab facility for a couple months and paid the bond for me to leave jail after my lawyer lowered it. I remember the bondwoman picking me up, bringing me to get something to eat and took me to a friend's house to change and clean up. I then went to visit my mother in the rehab facility. When I arrived, she hugged me very close and told me she loved me. I did not feel one ounce of disappointment from her instead I felt nothing but love. I then went home to start to get the house ready for my mother's return. I remember my sister-in-law picking me up one day to take me to get something to eat. She then proceeded to tell me they were moving to the north permanently. It was in that moment, that I felt lost and like I had been abandoned. I just got out of jail, my mother was at a rehab facility, my sister was living with her father and my brother who was the closest thing I had to a dad was leaving. There was no one there to help me process emotions, so I kept everything inside and went home again to finish getting ready for my mother's return.

I began to hang out with the same friends who did drugs shortly after I was released from jail. I decided to give drugs one last try. It was then in that moment, that I was repulsed by the drugs and hated every moment of being high. The next day after the drugs wore off, I realized that I had been completely delivered from them. I knew it had happened in jail when I heard about Jesus! I decided right then I would never try drugs again or hang out with those people and made it a point to never seen them again.

Chapter 3

The Struggle Continues

After jail, I was placed on a year of probation and I attended two different drug rehabilitation centers. I did decide to try to go back to college but my transcripts from the college I dropped out of followed me wherever I went. It made it exceedingly difficult to get any financial aid. I attended college and started working in the mall at a girls clothing store. I ended up meeting a guy in the mall who was from Israel. My best friend at the time and I began hanging out with him and some other of his friends. Of course, I was drinking heavily on a consistent basis and really could not go out with my friends without a drink.

In this time, I had convinced myself I could not get pregnant ever again. My relationship with this guy advanced to being sexual and again I ended up getting pregnant. I instantly went back to what I knew which was having an abortion. The guy I was seeing did not want me to have an abortion and wanted to get married. That was something I did not want so I started to push him away like I had always done everyone else.

I ended up having a second abortion and ruined the relationship with the guy and never saw him again. It was in this time I began to get severely depressed and started experienced significant fatigue. I ended up going to my doctor and they put me on depressions medication and anxiety medication. Little did I know, everything that was happening to me was related to the trauma of having the abortions and carrying around that burden for so many years. I ended up having to drop out of the second college because I could not function or focus in class.

A couple years went by and I did decide again to go back to college and work toward a degree in Criminal Justice at a community college. In college, I would still go through periods of depression, anxiety, and chronic fatigue. I was still going out, partying, and drinking with older groups of people. I remember one night; I was hanging out with a guy I met, and he probably was one of the most verbally abusive people I have ever met. Of course, I was always drawn to bad men because my lack of an earthly father in my life and because of all the abuse that I had experienced. We went to a bar and then went back to his house to hang out. At his house, he fixed me a drink and the next thing I remember I was waking up gasping for air with him taking my clothes off me. I knew in that moment that he had drugged me and was going to rape me. I grabbed my things and ran out of there as fast as I could. I know to this day it was the Lord who woke me up and protected me. I told my family and friends what had happened, and it was as if no one believed me and did not think this was a big deal. So again, I kept everything inside concerning what had happened and went on with my life.

My freshman year at the community college, I met a man who would become my husband. He was in the Air Force, was exceedingly kind and did genuinely nice things for me. This is something I was not accustomed to at all. Of course, my whole life all I had known was abusive men and thought that was what I needed. There were many times I tried to get rid of him because he was too nice. I tried my best to push him away as I had always done everyone else. I thought, why would someone want to love me, I am a broken mess. I never thought anything good about myself but no matter how hard I tried, I could not get rid of him and I ended up falling in love with him. We dated for six months, were engaged for six months, and ended up eloping after that.

He then began traveling around the world for the military and there was a lot of separation. I refused to move with him because I felt I needed to keep caring for my mother because that was all I had ever known. The separation put a huge strain on our marriage, and we fought constantly. We were always talking about getting a divorce. I thought is this what marriage is supposed to be like. It did not seem like anyone else we knew was happy in their marriage either. We thought this was only normal behavior. Little did I know we were carrying all the baggage of life's hurts into our marriage.

I graduated from college and took a job right away at a title company, which had nothing to do with my degree. I never felt good enough to pursue my career and was always listening to the voice in my head that told me I would never get a job, that no one would want me and that I was not good enough. I worked for the title company for five years. During that time, when I returned from a trip to Texas, I started to feel ill. I started to experience chronic fatigue like never before. I started seeing a couple doctors who told me they could not find anything wrong and it was all in my head. This went on for a full year and I ended up seeing over thirty-one doctors and even went to the Mayo Clinic in Minnesota. By that time, I was experiencing debilitating symptoms like anxiety, stroke, low blood pressure, weakness, chronic pain, sensitivity to light and sound, insomnia, weight loss, muscle wasting etc. I had to take a couple months off from work because I could not function at all. My brother flew down from Connecticut to take care of me for a couple weeks. It got so bad I literally felt like I was going to die. I remember I overslept one day, my mom came in to find me and cried because she thought I was dead. I would lie down at night and be so fearful I would never wake up again. In that moment, I felt nothing but darkness. I had lost all hope and thought no one could help me.

Chapter 4

A Fresh Start

It was October of 2012, when one of my family members invited my husband and I to attend a church, where they were doing a production called Beyond the Grave. I really did not know what it was about but decided my husband and I would attend. After attending, I realized it was a reproduction of the school shooting at Columbine. They showed the people who were shot and killed and if they went to heaven or hell. I will be completely honest; it was the scariest thing I had ever seen. It really shook me to my core, and I began to ask myself where was I going? It certainly was not heaven, so it had to be hell. I thought this is it, I am going to die, and I will go to hell. They gave an altar call at the end of the production to be born again and to believe in Jesus. In that moment, I decided I was going to surrender for the first time in my life and give my life to Jesus. I needed help; I could not do this on my own anymore. It was not working. What could I lose at this point?

My husband decided to give his life to Jesus too.

I remember standing up there saying a prayer and asking the Lord to forgive me for my sins. I confessed I believed He was the one who died for me and I choose to follow Him with all my heart. It was in that moment that I felt a heaviness lift off me for the first time in my life. I felt like it was going to be a fresh start, but I had no idea what to do next and no idea what God had in store for me.

After Beyond the Grave, my husband and I started attending the same church that held the production. My mother and youngest brother already attended there, and it seemed fitting since that is where we both were born again. For the next several months, I began coming to church regularly on Sundays to hear the Word. I really did not know what I was supposed to be doing as a Christian but knew I should be coming to church.

It was toward the end of the year,

when I decided I would try to see one last doctor in hopes of him helping me. My friend suggested a doctor in town, I called to make an appointment with him, but they said he was not seeing new patients and referred me to his colleague in the same clinic. I thought to myself, sure, I will see him, what could it hurt? Little did I know that God was already working on my behalf!

January rolled around and it was time for me to go to my doctor's appointment. Honestly, I do not think I went to the appointment with much hope. I arrived at the appointment and told the doctor what all had been going on with me physically for the last year. He looked at me and said, "have you ever been tested for Lyme disease?" I thought to myself, here we go again. A doctor had tested me for Lyme disease in the beginning and everything came back negative, so they said I did not have it. Later that year I saw a rheumatologist who tested me for Lyme

41

disease, and it came back positive, but they convinced me it was a false positive. Little did I know that a false positive is extremely rare, and it is exceedingly rare to get a positive with the standard test that the CDC uses. I told my doctor all of this and told him there was no way I had Lyme disease because of what all I had been told. After all, I believed they knew what they were talking about and had my best interest at heart. He proceeded to tell me all my symptoms I was experiencing lined up with Lyme disease and it was difficult to get a positive test or diagnosis because most doctors are not well versed in it. He then told me his dad was a forester and had been diagnosed with Lyme disease. He also had a doctor friend who was a Lyme Literate Medical Doctor and he had learned under him about Lyme disease.

It that moment I broke down and cried, God was helping me and making a way for me! What I thought was amazing was that I did not even ask God to help me. When I became His child at Beyond the Grave, I believe He already started to go to work on my behalf because He loves me that much!

The doctor started me on doxycycline right away to do the Lyme disease tests out of Palo Alto, California, which is more sensitive than the CDC tests. He said we needed to start taking the doxycycline to start killing off the spirochetes to get the immune system to produce a response for the tests to be accurate. It was two weeks later when I came back for the results. The tests were not completely positive, but the doctor said it was positive enough for him to make a diagnosis and with symptoms as well. He wanted to start me on doxycycline right away. He told me the treatment would be the equivalent to chemotherapy. I thought in that moment, "let's do this and kill this thing!" How hard could this be? Little did I know how difficult the treatment would be.

Just a couple weeks into the treatment, I felt worse than ever. Apparently, the antibiotics attack the bacteria and then the bacteria produce a die off or herxhiemer reaction, which floods your body with toxins. Most people who tests positive for Lyme disease also have issues with methylation and they need to take vitamins to support methylation and detox all the toxins out of the body. I remember laying in the shower and telling my husband I wanted to die, that is how bad it was. I thought this was going to be easy, but it certainly was not. I remember going to work and throwing up in the bathroom in secret almost every day from the medication. Everything seemed to have gotten worse. I started losing more weight, I had no appetite, horrible fatigue and it was so hard to maintain my workload at my job. I finally had to meet with my boss to have a reduction in my weekly hours just to try to maintain my job to pay for treatment. I remember most days; I would have to leave work and head over to the doctor's office to get IV Glutathione to help detox all the toxins just so I could function.

I went through this treatment every day for just under one year when I hit a plateau. My husband and I met with the doctor to discuss why this was happening. He told us there could be more infections but his knowledge after this point became somewhat limited. I remember going home and turning on the television and seeing a doctor on the news who was in a debate with an IDSA doctor regarding the controversy of Lyme disease. I was extremely impressed with the doctor and said to my husband, "we should look him up and see where he is, maybe they are taking patients." I tell you God is so good!

My husband is from upstate New York and at that time, we would travel up there once a year to see our families in New York and Connecticut. When we looked him up, we saw that his office was in upstate New York just one hour from my husband's family. We could not believe it! At that time, we had planet tickets to travel to New York to see our families for Christmas. I told my husband I am going to give their clinic a call and see if they are taking any patients for the week we are there. Now normally the week of Christmas most places are closed, and doctors are not usually seeing patients. I called their office, told them the situation and when we would be coming up there to visit. I could not believe it when they told me they had an opening with the doctor two days before Christmas. I knew God was working on our behalf and I knew that we were supposed to see this doctor as the next step.

I asked them for the fees for the Lyme Literate Medical Doctor and they were hefty. I decided to go ahead and make the appointment despite the fact we did not have the money to pay for it. My husband and I at the time did not have much extra money and we had already begun to go into debt from the illness. We said a prayer about going and for the money to pay for the visit. It was within a couple weeks that we received a refund check in the mail from our escrow and insurance policy. We also had money come in from reward points in my bank account. I remember adding up all the money and could not believe it when it literally added up to the dollar that we needed for the first appointment.

It was December 2013; we were on our way to New York. We arrived at the doctor's office and I will never forget how kind they were to me. They took me back and began running tests right away. The doctor came in and spent a long of time just talking to me and trying to understand everything that had transpired. I told him how many doctors I had seen before him and he said he has seen patients who have seen much more and literally come in with a suitcase of medical records. We were impressed by the knowledge of the doctor and how much he cared for his patients. The visit was very intensive and by the end I was quite exhausted. I think I was there for a total of four hours or more getting tests. They ended up running over $10,000 in lab work that day, started me on IV Glutathione plus a detox shake and did at least a $1000 worth of labs that were not covered by insurance. When we went to the checkout, we paid the $1283 for the first visit and walked out of there with $1400 in vitamins to start treatment. They told us we would come back once a year in person and would do phone consults every 4-6 weeks as needed to check in with the doctor. The telephone consults were $350 each and were not covered by insurance, neither were the vitamins or the initial visit. We really did not know what we were getting into financially or how we would pay for it, but we knew we had to do this to get me better. This was what we believed God for.

Three to four weeks later all the labs came back, and I scheduled a follow up phone consultation with the doctor. He proceeded to tell me there were four other tick-borne diseases that had come back positive. Those included Rocky Mountain Spotted Fever, Bartonella, Babesia, Mycoplasma and there were also elevated levels of Epstein Barr Virus and other viruses in my system. They wanted to start treatment right away and started me on five different antibiotics at the same time. They also instructed me to take a ton of vitamins every day and tinctures to detox the toxins from the treatments and die off.

I honestly think that at that point I was beyond overwhelmed. We made an appointment with my doctor back home who agreed to work in conjunction with the Lyme Literate Medical Doctor to help treat me and support me. I remember sitting in his office and having a break down. He said to me this is a good thing, this is what we thought was going on and now we know how to treat it and move forward. In that moment, I thought to myself I do not know if I can keep going, the first treatment was hard enough. Will this ever get better? My husband and I decided that day that we would move forward and start the treatment.

To say the first treatment was difficult was an understatement, this treatment was crippling. We were now killing off five different diseases at the same time and killing viruses. There were days that I felt like I could not get out of bed. I remember they told me I would have to start working out as part of the treatment and I thought, "Okay sure, I can do that". When my husband took me to the gym, they told me it would be best for me to use the circuit training machines. I remember on a level one I could hardly lift it;

it was the most difficult thing; I had lost all my strength.

As part of the treatment, we also bought an infrared sauna to do sauna detox treatments in the home. We also did Epsom salt and baking soda baths and continued the IV Glutathione treatments. We started doing those treatments at home and my husband would administer them. My whole day and life were consumed by taking medicine, vitamins and doing detox therapies. At one point, I had to write out the daily schedule of medication because there was so much to take. The sheet I had written out literally had me taking something every fifteen minutes after I woke up until I went to bed. I remember counting out all the pills and it totaled out to be around eighty pills a day plus eight different tinctures.

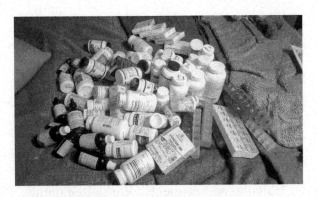

Pills I was taking every day

I believe it was by the Grace of God that He helped me to do it all and to keep going.

Chapter 5

Believing for the Impossible

We continued through treatment with this doctor for another year and a half. It was in 2015, that our church began to promote a healing crusade they were hosting called Freedom Crusade. Now I had been going to the same church since I was born again for the last three years but I had never attended one of the Freedom Crusades because I was so sick. It was hard enough just to go to church on Sunday morning and try to focus on the preaching and the screen with the scriptures because it was difficult to read. As we got closer to the crusade, I began to hear about the healing that Jesus paid for us when he went to the cross. When I was born again, I had no idea that Jesus was a Healer and that was available for me. After all, the doctors were telling me this was chronic, that there was no cure and that I would have to go through treatment forever.

It was July; I decided to go to the first night of the crusade, which was a worship night. I will never forget that one of the girls in the choir spoke and told us to come every night believing God for our miracle, that He had done a miracle in her life at one of the past crusades. It was hard for me to stand for extended periods of time and being in a large group of people was overstimulating for me and would wear me out but I decided in that moment I would come expecting God to heal me!

The second night was the first night, they preached for quite some time and I remember hearing a lot about healing. I heard about how Jesus's body was broken for me so I could be healed and that I did not have to live a life of sickness. The preacher said Jesus bore every sickness, pain, and disease in His body so I could be free. I remember thinking to myself; I can be free of this? The doctor has said I cannot, but God's Word is saying that I can! It was such great news to me! At the time of the crusade, I had lost so much weight I was under a hundred pounds and looked like a skeleton.

I weighted under 100 lbs. during treatment

I thought I could not keep doing this; this is no way to live life. I literally came to that crusade broken but I had faith in me rise up to believe God could do a miracle in my body. It was the next night that I came back and heard the Word concerning healing. I was so full of faith I told myself I was going to be healed that night!

A move of the Holy Spirit fell in

that place and the pastors there began saying if you need healing in your body to come down to the front, we want to lay hands on you for healing. I knew in that moment I was going down and I was going to be healed! It is hard to explain but I had absolute faith rise up in my Spirit that I was going to be healed and I would never be sick again. I ran down to the front and waited in line with everyone to receive healing. I will never forget the pastor coming over to me. He looked at me and asked me what it was, and I said it was Lyme disease. He said okay and began to pray over me taking authority over the disease. He then laid hands on me, I felt the power of God come over me, and I cried and cried. He stayed with me and kept laying hands on me and then I felt a peace come over me. He looked at me and said, "You are free today, go and claim your healing!" I knew in that moment it was the Spirit of God talking to me. I received that Word from the Lord and I felt in my body that I was healed.

After the crusade, there was a table out in the lobby with all the books the pastor had for sale. There was a 365 Days of Healing Devotional the pastor had wrote and I knew I was supposed to get that book. I asked my husband to buy it for me even though at this point we were severely in debt from all the treatment, probably $40,000 or more. My husband gladly bought it for me, and I began to read it every day. The next day I woke up and my body had begun to swell in odd places. We had always blessed the medicine I took, and I had never experienced any side effects the whole length of treatment. I put in an emergency call to the Lyme doctor and he instructed me to quit taking the antibiotics that my body was rejecting the medication. Did you hear what he said? My body was rejecting the medication. We knew in that moment I was healed and that my body no longer needed that medication. They decided to move me over onto Chinese herbs and vitamins, so I blessed those and took them every day.

That night we were back at the crusade and I remember they called out healing for people with chronic disease. My Mom looked at me and said that is you, you need to go down but I remember thinking to myself I do not need to go down, I am already healed, but I went down for my mother anyway! After the crusade was over, I began to read the healing devotional every day and it began to teach me the Word of God concerning healing. I had no idea what all the Word of God said about healing. There were many misconceptions I had in my mind concerning healing and the will of God. Over the years, people had told me a lot of incorrect things about who God was. They said God did this, he is trying to teach you something and He will receive glory through you being sick and so on. I mean a lot of wrong thinking. God is not any of those things at all. Those people do not know who God is or what His Word even says.

One month later I was scheduled to fly to New York to check in with the Lyme doctor. I remember waiting there for the doctor and when he came in, he could not believe his eyes. He said to me, "You have put on a good bit of weight, you have color in your skin, you seem like you are in good spirits and you look really good." At the time, I did not tell him that I had been healed at a crusade. I was nervous and did not know what he would say, and I wanted to protect my healing. He instructed me to continue taking the Chinese herbs and vitamins and check in periodically through telephone consultation.

I continued to take the herbs and vitamins as instructed for the next year. It was a couple weeks before the crusade when the Lyme doctor wanted to retest for all the diseased.

I had been standing on my healing for the last year and was getting better and better every day. I remember asking people to pray for me for negative results and I wanted to share my testimony at the Freedom Crusade to help other people.

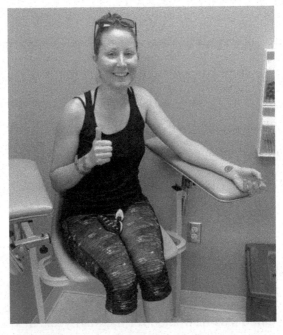

Day I was retested for Lyme Disease, etc.

That day I went for the testing, I read in my devotional this scripture on June 21st,

2016. "Then Jesus answered and said unto her, O Woman, great is thy faith: be in unto thee even as thou will. And her daughter was made whole from that very hour." Matthew 15:28

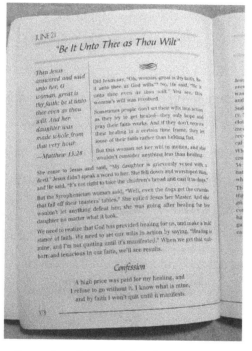

Devotional I read the day of testing

I then went to the lab and told the lab tech I had been healed as they were retesting me. She shared this same scripture with me and then a family member shared the same scripture with me after the test was complete. I know God was speaking to me that I had been totally healed by my faith in Him! Praise God!

Right before the eve of the crusade, we got the results back online and they were all negative! I told one of my pastors and she asked me to type up my testimony quickly for the Freedom Crusade. They shared my testimony on the opening night, and I believe it was such a blessing for people to hear and helped build their faith to receive their miracle. That year at the Freedom Crusade, I received the Holy Spirt and the prayer language of speaking in tongues! God is so good that every year around that time He does something supernaturally for me! Little did I know God was doing so much more for me in the way of healing and restoration!

(see next page for picture)

Test results for Lyme Disease, etc.

Chapter 6

The Healing Journey Begins

It was in early 2017, I had a conversation with one of my pastors. I told her I knew I was healed but I still was dealing with some fatigue and did not feel like I had much joy in my life. She said to me, "Joy you have been through a lot, but have you ever dealt with any of it?" I said to her, "deal with it? How do you deal with it?" I had no clue what that meant, after all, I had never dealt with anything my whole life, I just always kept it inside and kept going. I was a survivor remember. Life groups were about to start at the church, and she recommended me doing a life group called Ditch the Baggage. She told me it really helped her to heal from some things and she knew it would help me. I asked her if it was going to be like counseling and all you would do is sit around and cry. I had seen a counselor in the past, that is all we did, and nothing ever was truly healed. She told me it was not going to be like that, but it was going to be under the counsel of the Holy

Spirit. I thought to myself, why not?

In early 2017, I signed up for the Ditch the Baggage group. I went for the interview and was told one of the girls from church whom God connected me to was leading one of the groups. I told them I wanted to be part of that specific group. It is funny how God really puts everything in place for you. I came to the group with the expectation to be healed from going through an illness but as I was going through the group, I would find out God had a bigger plan to do much more for me! On my first day of the group, I did not really know what to expect. I had never been much of an emotional person, very rarely cried and never spent a lot of time around females and this group was solely women. I remember I told myself I was not going to cry! On the first day, I was the first person to cry! I had been holding everything in for so long that in that moment everything just came out and I felt such a release from what all I had been hiding for so many years. God really does have a sense of humor!

I remember the first part of the group was about remembering events that have happened in our lives. Memories have always been something hard for me but as I went through this book I was able to remember things that occurred in my life that were hurtful to me or made an impact on me but there were also good memories as well.

Then came the hard part, which was healing the hurts. That was something I never ever wanted to have to do in my life. I never even knew they could be healed, I thought things just happened to you and that is how life is and you just move on and keep going. Despite being hesitant, I welcomed in the Lord to heal my heart. Through this group I heard that Jesus came to free me and when I heard I could be free I decided I wanted all of it, I wanted to be totally free and walk in everything God had for me for my life.

I took personal time with the Lord outside of the group to start going through hurtful memories and events as the book instructed. I would go to the Lord in prayer regarding the hurt and would ask Him to give me the strength to face it and process through it. I would then release the memory to Him and ask Him to come in and heal that memory for me. It was not a fun time, it was very emotional and painful, but the healing and freedom that came made it all worth it.

There were many memories that I went back and processed with the Lord and in those memories, He showed me that He was there with me. That was amazing for me to see that the Lord did not do those things to me, but He was always there with me. One memory was when the guy I was seeing drugged me and tried to rape me. When the Lord took me through that memory, I saw that He was there, and He was the one that caused me to wake up so I could escape safely. He protected me in that situation even when I was not living for Him. I began to realize that He had always been with me in every situation and had never forsaken me, even when I was not living for Him.

Chapter 7

Changed in A Moment

One of the hardest things for me going through the life group was forgiveness. When we came to forgiveness, I did not want to do it, but I had to remember the process He was taking me through was for my good. He was trying to help me and heal me, not hurt me in any way, so I trusted Him.

Some of the memories were not difficult for me to forgive, like the guy who tried to molest me when I was a young girl. There were other memories that were quite difficult to forgive. One instance was when my mother had a stroke. As I was going through that memory with the Lord, I realized I had been mad at Him for a long time and I thought He had done that to my mother. I had to make the decision to forgive Him and chose to believe what His Word says about Him. I then had to make the decision to forgive myself. The Lord showed me I was blaming myself for what had happened to my mother and that is why I always felt I had to stay and care for her and could never move to be with my husband. I was always trying to make up for what I thought I had done wrong.

I will never forget, during the life group, my husband and I traveled to Houston, Texas to attend Jesus Image Conference with a group of friends. A friend of my husband mentioned it and we decided to go not knowing what all would happen there. It was a three-day conference with speakers throughout the day and an afternoon outreach. I think it was the second day the Holy Spirit fell in that church where the conference was, and everyone started travailing in the Spirit with groanings. I had never encountered anything like it; God was birthing something in that place that I believe would later go to launch a revival, which I believe we are on the cusp of right now.

The presence of God stayed very thick in that place the entire time. One of the speakers, shared about the love of Jesus and how we should forgive others as He has forgiven us. They also shared that if we do not forgive others, we are keeping that person captive essentially and they need to be released. It was so powerful; I felt the Holy Spirit all over me and for the first time it made sense to me.

In that moment, I heard the Lord say, "go call your father." I had not spoken to my father very much my entire life and the last time I saw him was a couple years prior to that when he came down, we had dinner and I really was not in a place to forgive or build a relationship as I still had my walls up. I was also going through a severe illness. I did not have the strength to try to deal with it at the time. I heard again, "go call your father." Then, "go call your father, go call your father, call your father right now." I told my husband I had to step outside, and I would be back. I knew the Lord wanted me to call my father, forgive him and release him.

All these years I had been in un-forgiveness toward my earthly father because he had hurt me, and I had felt abandoned and unloved. I had convinced myself all those years that I had forgiven him, but I really had not and was carrying around a heavy burden. As I got outside, I dialed the phone and my father's wife answered the phone. I told her I needed to talk to my father. She told me he was busy working on the truck with someone, but she could have him call me back. I told her I needed to talk to him now, that it was especially important and if I did not talk to him now, I never would. She put him on the phone and honestly I do not know what all I said other than I forgive you for what you said and did to me and I have to release you now. I did tell him I wanted to have a relationship with him, and I asked him to forgive me for not forgiving him.

On the other side of the phone was nothing but silence and I was crying my eyes out. I do not know what else was said but I know the Holy Spirit had spoken through me as well. My father finally said I do not know what to say and I told him I was at a conference, that God was moving and doing amazing things and had instructed me to call him. We got off the phone and while my father did not say anything to me, I felt such a burden lifted off me and I felt a peace and a healing like I have never have.

I went back into the conference and listened to the rest of the speakers. I remember the last night there they were talking about wanting Jesus. I heard Jesus preached in a way I had never ever heard before. It was the love of Jesus, His desire for us and it burned in me. The Holy Spirit fell in that place. I told the Lord I want all of you Lord. Little did I know what I was really asking for. I started to let my Spirit just yield to the Lord and I felt myself start to almost leave my body. I began crying out so loud you could hear it through the church. The next thing I know the man preaching called me to the front, but I could not walk. Two gentlemen came and got me and took me up to the front. I was so overwhelmed by the power of God that I did not even know how I had got up to the front. The man then blew on me and the fire of God came upon me so much that my whole body became to shake. I started crying out because it felt like I was on fire. My whole body was convulsing, and I was in so much pain from the Fire of God.

Eventually I made it down to the floor where I laid for hours convulsing and crying. I saw a vision of my husband and I walking with a little boy through a beautiful garden with gold dust all around. What I did not know until the next day was my husband had a vision at the same time, I was laying on the floor in a vision of an angel handing him a baby. In that moment, I knew the Lord was burning everything out of my life that would hold me back. I also knew God was birthing something but also God was going to bless us with a child and restore the past. I felt in that moment that I truly died with Him and every desire that I had was burned up.

After hours of lying on the floor, my husband came to pick me up. By then most of the people had already left the conference. I was under the Fire of God so much that I could barely walk, and I could not talk. It was hard to talk for days after the conference. I remember the next day at the hotel, I just sat in the window and cried because it was such a powerful and Holy moment unlike, I had ever experienced. It was in that moment, that everything in my life changed. It was in that moment that I knew the Fire of God had baptized me. I left there forever changed by Jesus!

(see next page for picture)

Jesus Image Conference

As I returned home, I felt such a shift take place in my thinking, my attitude, and my life. Months earlier, my husband called me while I was in Arizona and told me he felt he had a call of God on his life to preach. I remember I was totally caught off guard and said to him, "well there goes our lives." I did not want anything to do with ministry and certainly did not feel called, but after my return home, my attitude changed greatly. I still was under the Fire of God for days and was on fire so much that I called my husband and told him I wanted to pack up and move to

Florida to go to Jesus school. I am sure he thought I had lost my mind but, in that moment, I knew I was called to ministry too. In that moment, I had gone from broken to chosen!

I remember discussing with my leaders what had taken place and that I felt called and wanted to leave and start ministering. They instructed me that there is a time of preparation and then a time of being sent. I valued their wisdom and decided to wait and see what God had in store for me.

I also discussed the forgiveness that took place between my father and I, I told my leader that it did bother me that my father did not say anything to me. She shared with me that she too had sent a letter to her father and it was months later before he responded to her. She instructed me that maybe he just needed some time to process the information and for me not to be upset but just wait, so that is what I did. I focused on finishing the life group that I was in.

As I was finishing the life group, I remember the Church started advertising for ministry school again. They had advertised for it before and I would always go up, get the packet from the woman, and then wonder why I had gotten the packet because I did not want to go to ministry school at all. Remember I said the Lord has a sense of humor! However, after the conference, I knew I was called, and I went up to her and got the ministry school packet again. This time I had a desire to go to ministry school and knew I was called. I remember attending the open house where you could come and check out of the school and sit in on a class. I told the Lord prior to coming that I really did not feel like I belonged anywhere after coming back from the conference. It was there during the class, that the Lord spoke to me and said, "This is where you belong." I said okay Lord and I went and signed up that night for ministry school.

Day I signed up for School of Ministry

Shortly after singing up, I finished the life group and they threw a nice graduation party for us. For the first time in my life I felt like I was starting to walk in the freedom that Jesus provided for me.

Chapter 8

God's Not Done

It was a couple weeks later when my leaders asked if I would not mind coming by her office at the church. I went and as I came in the room and sat down, I could tell it was serious. I thought to myself what is wrong with them, what did I do? They proceeded to bring up the fact that I had confessed about having two abortions at the life group and told me they had an abortion recovery group available they thought could really help me. I remember sitting there, just hearing the word abortion almost made me black out. I told them it was not something I really wanted to do but I trusted them that they were bringing this up to help me and not hurt me, so I decided to do it.

It never occurred to me as I was going through the life group that I needed to heal that area of my life or maybe I just was not ready. Can you see God here working on my behalf for total restoration? He knew I was not ready, and He knew to put me in the right life group with the right leaders who knew about this abortion group and could guide and support me through it.

My first day at the abortion recovery group was a little awkward and I will be honest I really did not want to be there. Healing is not hard, it is the process of healing that can be difficult, and that is where many people have trouble. They want to be free, but they do not want to go through the process God is asking them to go through. I remember during that session I said the word abortion aloud for the first time since I had the abortions when I was seventeen years old. I put my head on the table and just cried and cried. I could feel God already breaking chains off me and healing me. Most of the time, we just need to expose something out loud and then it is no longer a secret and the enemy cannot use it against us.

I went through this abortion recovery group for ten weeks right before the time to start ministry school. In the recovery group, I learned a lot about the character of God and who He really is. I learned how to process emotions surrounding the abortions. I learned it was okay to be angry in that moment for what had happened, the people who had lied to me and the pain it had caused me. He showed me how to release those emotions and let Him come in and heal them. I also learned how to forgive my mother, the man who got me pregnant, the clinic where I had the abortions, my friend who took me, people who made me feel bad because of what I had done and most importantly God and myself. Forgiving myself for having the abortions was probably the hardest thing. I learned in the group that God forgave me and set me free when Jesus went to the cross. The only thing I needed to do was accept it and not condemn myself.

While I was going through the abortion recovery group God really did a work for me concerning my marriage. My husband called me one day from Texas and told me he had fallen in love with me all over again. It felt as if our marriage was being renewed and we were starting over with a fresh start. God also restored the relationship between my mother and me. I was able to speak to my mother for the first time about the abortion, forgive her, and ask her to forgive me. Our relationship from then on has only increased in closeness and joy. In addition, a month or so after returning from the conference where I forgave my father, he called me and told me thank you for forgiving him, that he forgave me too and he too wanted to work on having a relationship together. God is truly amazing! God was working total restoration in my life!

I remember the last day of the group was by far the hardest thing I had ever done in my life. I had to get the names of my two children from God and write them a letter. Their names are Elizabeth and Samuel.

Writing the letter was difficult; I do not think I have ever cried so hard in my life. They played the song Natalie Grant's "Clean" and handed me two baby dolls that had been sewn. I held my two children in my arms for the first time ever, read them the letter, and asked them to forgive me for what I had done. I released them to the Lord and asked Jesus to take care of them for me. I remember in that moment hearing the laughter of children. God is so good that He would comfort me like that in that moment. They gave me flowers, a bracelet to remember and a candle to light in honor of my children. It was a beautiful moment of forgiveness, freedom, and the love of the Father.

After the group, I felt for the first time in my life I was totally free and unburdened. I felt I had a new life and could start over. I also felt a desire for conceiving children again, something I had never experienced because I always blamed myself for what I had done. My husband and I agreed to start believing God for children. How amazing is that? Only Jesus Christ could do that for someone. I knew the past was behind me and when the devil tried to bring it up, I would remind him of what the Word of God said and what God did for me. I left the group ready for the next season of my journey, ministry school.

Chapter 9

Restoration

It was now August of 2017 and ministry school was starting. I was so excited about what God was doing in my life and could not wait to get to class to learn more about Him and the Word of God. God connected me with a girl from church prior to school and we both signed up and went through school together. We sat right next to each other for two years. God is so good that He gives us people to help support and encourage us along our way.

As I started ministry school, I decided to move out of my mother's house into an apartment. I did not know how I was going to pay for it, but God! One day I received a check in the mail from my old job for a retirement account worth over $12,000. My husband was still living in Texas on military orders and paying for a house there. God had graced me with the finances to move into an apartment and with a wonderful Christian roommate who I grew to be remarkably close to and helped support me through ministry school. I also was able to pay off a significant portion of the debt we had incurred from treatment prior to being healed. Praise God!

Ministry school was simply amazing and life changing! All our teachers imparted such knowledge to us in those two years. The presence of God was so strong during our worship hour and there were such amazing impartations of the Holy Spirit. School of ministry was not easy though; the enemy was on the prowl for two years and tried to bring many attacks against us, but we stood strong and kept ourselves in worship and in prayer.

I remember during my first year of school of ministry God was really working in our lives. My husband felt led to get ordained to be a minister, so he applied the year prior for ordination. The application was approved, we traveled to a minister's conference in June we are always part of, and I was able to be with my husband as he was ordained.

My husband's ordination with Tracy & Lori

Harris of Harvest International Ministries

That moment was such a joyous moment to see what God was doing, not only in my life, but in my husband's as well.

In July, I attended the Freedom Crusade again. During this time, the Lord had instructed me to come off all medications and supplements, which I had not taken in almost a year at that point. I felt led to throw everything out. I also felt led to contact the Lyme Doctor and tell them God had healed me and ask them to discharge me. I felt led to close that door and believe for total restoration. It was on the eve of the Beyond the Grave that I received the written letter from my doctor discharging me with blessings.

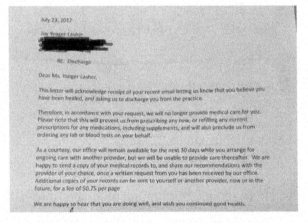

Discharge letter from Lyme Specialist

I went to the crusade and on the last night, I went down to the front for healing and as my pastor prayed over me, he spoke out, by the

Spirit of God, total restoration over me. In that moment, I received it and I knew I had been totally restored. Restoration is not just your body. It is your finances, your dreams, your marriage, children, family, relationships, etc. Restoration is everything the enemy tried to steal from you.

After the crusade, I returned to ministry school in August. While I was in ministry school, I think the most important class I took for me personally was the class on my identity in Christ. We had to write out all the scriptures in the New Testament that had in Christ, in Whom, and in Him. There are literally hundreds of those scriptures and to read all of them and write them out really begins to tell you who you are in Christ Jesus.

While I was in ministry school, God spoke to me my calling. I knew my calling was healing and to help women find freedom. God started opening doors concerning that area and started using me to help other people.

I was asked by my life group leader to lead a Keys to Freedom group which is the newer version of Ditch the Baggage. I then also was asked to lead a life group with one of my pastors which would help teach other women who they are in Christ, their calling and how to help others with their calling.

One of my pastors and I leading a life group

I was also able to share my freedom testimony

including the abortion testimony with hundreds of women at a women's conference at our Church.

Sharing my testimony at a women's conference

I was able to serve at the Beyond the Grave production at my Church, which is the same production I got saved at. I was able to minister to people for salvation. It was such an honor to be part of Beyond the Grave and be able to minister to people! My second year in school of ministry I was asked to serve as one of the team leads for the women's conference to host the Mercy Multiplied girls. I traveled to Monroe, Louisiana to visit with the girls there while one of my pastors preached. I hosted them when they came to the conference and was able to pour into their lives in that time. God did some amazing things and opened doors for me without me having to try to open them.

In May 2019, I graduated with my class from School of Ministry with a 4.0 for both years. In that moment, I had such joy because God is so good that He literally redeemed all the years of college that I had failed, ruined my grades, and dropped out. He made everything new! Graduation was bittersweet because it was also my last night at

My mother and I at Ministry School
Graduation

church. I had been at this church for seven years where I had grown as a Christian. My husband had received orders for us to move to New Jersey and the military had approved the extension so I could graduate with my class. Our ministers prayed over us that night for our new season.

(see next page for picture)

One of our pastors praying over us the night of graduation

The next morning, we hit the road on our new adventure for New Jersey!

Moving to New Jersey

When we arrived in New Jersey, one week

later we signed the paperwork on our first home together that we were believing the Lord for!

Bought our first home together

In July 2019, the Lord blessed me with a trip to New York City for my birthday. My husband and I were blessed with Legend tickets to a Yankee's game on my birthday. My husband is a huge Yankees fan and is from New York. We knew it was the Lord who blessed us with the tickets which made it the best birthday ever!

Yankee Stadium on my birthday

Then in November, my husband traveled to France to finish up learning French for the military. I bought a plan ticket and flew over to France to meet him in Paris. Exactly seven years ago to the day, my husband and I were supposed to travel to France and Rome to celebrate our anniversary. This was a trip I had always dreamed of taking my entire life. Shortly before the trip in 2012,

I grew ill and we had to cancel our trip. We never even thought again about taking the trip. God is amazing in how He put it all together for us! We traveled to Paris and Rome and celebrated our anniversary! I remember staring at the Eiffel Tower during the hourly night light show and just crying because God is so good! He restored everything in our lives!

Paris, France - Eiffel Tower

Paris, France - Louvre Museum, Mona Lisa

Rome, Italy – The Colosseum

Versailles, France - Palace of Versailles

Chapter 10

We are Just Getting Started

It is now May 2020; my husband and I have been in New Jersey for almost one year. God has supernaturally connected us to a Church here and we are both actively serving. The last ten months have been quite difficult for us not knowing what the next season would bring and when that would start. It has been a time of waiting upon the Lord and knowing direction will come. We are now in the midst of a global pandemic with COVID-19 and we have been at home under stay at home orders for 40 days. In this time, we have pressed into God in worship and prayer. This book has been birthed out of time spent with the Lord in a season of waiting. We have also felt led to minister on Facebook to two different groups of people. My husband has also written a book in this time called "Walking in Fullness." We are about to start co-writing a book on healing. We also have some visions the Lord has shown us concerning outreach ministry in our community.

I know in this time God is doing a work in every believer and bringing new believers to Christ. This is a great time of seeking God and coming out of our comfort zones as believers. I believe there is a mighty move of God coming in this season that will produce a great revival around the world and the third great awakening. God is calling Christian to rise up in their prayer closet and pray for this nation and for the revival that is to come. I believe there will be a great outpouring of His Spirit on believers to propel them and set them on fire to bring the Gospel around the globe.

I know in this time I was to write this book for you to help you receive healing and freedom through Jesus Christ and to be able to move into the fullness that God has for your life in this time that we are being called to rise up.

I felt led to share my story with you so

you could see the amazing work God did in my life and know that He wants to do it in your life too! All you have to do is BE WILLING! Say YES! It is your time to rise up! God is saying do not stay broken, you are CHOSEN!

Chapter 11

Your Journey Begins

Now your story begins! I have made this section for you so you can study out the Word of God concerning your healing and your freedom! Let the Word of God speak to you who you truly are and transform your life!

Salvation Prayer

If you are reading this book and have never given your life to Jesus, the first step to take in your faith if you have not already is to give your life to Jesus and be born again! The Word of God says, "That if you confess with your mouth the Lord Jesus and believe in your heart that God has raised Him from the dead, you will be saved. For with the heart one believes unto righteousness, and with the mouth confession is made unto salvation."

Rom 10:9-10

The way for us to receive Jesus, is to believe in our heart that He is Lord, was raised from the dead and confess it with our mouths. Let us say this prayer together out loud.

"I believe Jesus is the Son of God. I believe that Jesus bore all my sins in his body on the cross and He was bruised for my healing. He died for me on the cross and was raised from the dead so I can have eternal life. I believe Jesus is alive. Lord Jesus, please forgive me of all my sins and cleanse me of all unrighteousness. I believe in my heart and confess with my mouth that Jesus Christ is my Lord and Savior and I am born again. I ask you to fill me with your Holy Spirit. Thank you for saving me."

Congratulations on giving your life to Jesus Christ! Praise God! I know God is going to do a supernatural work in your life just like He did in mine. Let us jump right into scripture and find out what the Word of God says about us! Take time to meditate on what the Word says about you.

What Jesus Did for You

You Are a New Creation

"Therefore, if anyone is in Christ, he is a new creation; old things have passed away; behold, all things have become new."

II Cor 5:17

Did you know that the word new in the Greek text means recently made, fresh, and of a new kind? How amazing is that? You have a fresh start. You are NEW!

You Are Forgiven

"In Him we have redemption through

His blood, the forgiveness of sins, according
to the riches of His grace."

Eph 1:7

You have been forgiven of all your
sins through the blood of Jesus Christ! Some
people might say, "but you don't know what I
did." It does not matter what you did. Jesus
forgave Saul who was a murderer of
Christians. He raised up Saul, changed his
name to Paul and used him to preach the
Gospel. And he wrote a great deal of the New
Testament.

Let us look at the story of Lazarus.
In the story of Lazarus in John 11, Martha's
brother Lazarus had died. Jesus came to heal
him but was late in arriving. Lazarus had
been in the tomb for four days and the Bible
says there was a stench which means his body
was decomposing.

"Now when He had said these things,
He cried with a loud voice, "Lazarus, come

forth!" And he who had died came out bound hand and foot with graveclothes, and his face was wrapped with a cloth. Jesus said to them, "Loose him, and let him go."

John 11:43-44

Jesus raised Lazarus from the dead to illustrate that there is no one who is too far gone to be forgiven and raised to life with Him. Jesus also instructed Lazarus to take off the graveclothes which are the sins of the past.

You Have Eternal Life

"For God so loved the world that He gave His only begotten Son, that whoever believes in Him should not perish but have everlasting life."

John 3:16

You now have eternal life by believing in Jesus Christ!

He Does not Remember Your Sin

"As far as the east is from the west, so far has He removed our transgressions from us."

Psa 103:12

This scripture is saying that the Father does not remember our sin. It is as far is the east from the west. He holds no records of your wrongs.

There is no Condemnation in Christ Jesus

"There is therefore now no condemnation to those who are in Christ Jesus."

Rom 8:1

Remember God does not condemn us for our past so we should not either. If you mess up, remember you can ask for forgiveness. It is that simple!

"If we confess our sins, He is faithful and just to forgive us our sins and to cleanse us from all unrighteousness."

I John 1:9

He Has Made You Righteous

"For He made Him who knew no sin to be sin for us, that we might become the righteousness of God in Him."

You are now made righteous! Sin no longer defines you!

You Are Seated in Heavenly Places

"Even when we were dead in trespasses, made us alive together with Christ (by grace you have been saved), and raised us up together, and made us sit together in heavenly places in Christ Jesus."

Eph 2:5-6

You are now seated in heavenly places with Christ Jesus at the right hand of the Father.

Who You Are in Christ

You Are Blessed

"Who has blessed us with every spiritual blessing in the heavenly places in Christ."

Eph 1:3

You Are Chosen

"Just as He chose us in Him before the foundation of the world."

Eph 1:4

You Are Loved

"That we should be holy and without blame before Him in love."

Eph 1:4

You Are Adopted

"Having predestined us to adoption as sons by Jesus Christ to Himself."

Eph 1:5

You Are Accepted

"According to the good pleasure of His will, to the praise of the glory of His grace, by which He made us accepted in the Beloved."

Eph 1:6

You Are Redeemed

"In Him we have redemption through His blood."

Eph 1:7

You Are Forgiven

"The forgiveness of sins, according to the riches of His grace which made to abound toward us in all wisdom and prudence."

Eph 1:7

You Have an Inheritance

"In Him also we have obtained an inheritance, being predestined according to the purpose of Him who works all things according to the counsel of His will."

Eph 1:11

You Are Sealed by the Holy Spirit

"In Him you also trusted, after you heard the word of truth, the gospel of your salvation; in whom also, having believed, you were sealed with the Holy Spirit of promise, who is the guarantee of our inheritance until the redemption of the purchased possession, to the praise of His glory."

Eph 1:13

You Are Free

"Therefore if the Son makes you free, you shall be free indeed."

John 8:36

You Are Healed

"Who Himself bore our sins in His own body on the tree, that we, having died to sins, might life for righteousness – by whose stripes you were healed."

I Peter 2:24

Resources

Keys to Freedom by Nancy Alcorn
https://mercymultiplied.com/keys-to-freedom-study/

Forgiven and Set Free by Linda Cochrane
Available on Amazon

True Image, Walking In Your True Image by Lindsey Bussey
http://www.thisismytrueimage.com/

Walking In Fullness, Discovering All Jesus Has For You by Stephen Lasher
Available on Amazon

About the Author

After being born again in October 2012, the Lord took Joy on a journey of forgiveness, healing, freedom, and restoration. It is her calling to help others find freedom and healing through Jesus Christ. She graduated Word of Life School of Ministry in 2019 with an associate degree in Ministry. Her husband, Stephen Lasher, is an ordained minister under Harvest International Ministries. They both reside in New Jersey.

Contact

joylasherbooks@gmail.com

Notes

Notes

Notes

Notes

Notes